WAY TO GROW! GARDENING
COMPOSTING

by Rebecca Pettiford

pogo

Ideas for Parents and Teachers

Pogo Books let children practice reading informational text while introducing them to nonfiction features such as headings, labels, sidebars, maps, and diagrams, as well as a table of contents, glossary, and index.

Carefully leveled text with a strong photo match offers early fluent readers the support they need to succeed.

Before Reading

- "Walk" through the book and point out the various nonfiction features. Ask the student what purpose each feature serves.
- Look at the glossary together. Read and discuss the words.

Read the Book

- Have the child read the book independently.
- Invite him or her to list questions that arise from reading.

After Reading

- Discuss the child's questions. Talk about how he or she might find answers to those questions.
- Prompt the child to think more. Ask: Do you have a garden? If so, have you ever used compost? Did you make it yourself?

Pogo Books are published by Jump!
5357 Penn Avenue South
Minneapolis, MN 55419
www.jumplibrary.com

Library of Congress Cataloging-in-Publication Data

Pettiford, Rebecca, author.
 Composting / by Rebecca Pettiford.
   pages cm. – (Way to grow! Gardening)
 Includes index.
 ISBN 978-1-62031-229-2 (hardcover: alk. paper) –
 ISBN 978-1-62496-316-2 (ebook)
 1. Compost–Juvenile literature. I. Title. II. Series:
 Pettiford, Rebecca. Way to grow! Gardening.
 S661.P44 2015
 631.8'75–dc23
                                   2015000275

Series Editor: Jenny Fretland VanVoorst
Series Designer: Anna Peterson
Photo Researcher: Anna Peterson

Photo Credits: All photos by Shutterstock except:
Alamy, 6-7; Getty, 8, 9, 18-19; iStock, 3; SuperStock,
12-13; Thinkstock, 5, 10-11, 14, 15, 23.

Printed in the United States of America at
Corporate Graphics in North Mankato, Minnesota.

TABLE OF CONTENTS

CHAPTER 1

YOUR GARDEN'S BEST FRIEND

Plants need good soil to grow healthy and strong.

Did you know that soil has dead plants and animals in it? This is **organic matter**.

Compost is full of organic matter. Your garden will love it!

A well-made compost pile supplies the right amount of water and air so that **micro-organisms** can get to work. These **organisms** help break organic matter down into compost.

DID YOU KNOW?

Earthworms love compost, too. They help the soil by adding air to it when they tunnel through it. Healthy gardens have a lot of worms!

earthworm

CHAPTER 2

MAKING COMPOST

You can make your own compost pile. Use organic matter like leaves, paper, and table scraps.

Add water to it. Turn and mix it. This helps the pile stay wet. It also moves air through it.

When you make a pile,
you are making **humus**.

Humus is dead plant and animal
matter. It is high in **nitrogen**
and **carbon**.

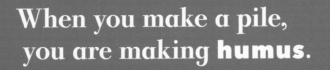

DID YOU KNOW?

When you make and use
compost, you are recycling.
This helps cut down on the
waste in **landfills**.

Matter that has a lot of nitrogen is often fresh and green. It includes green grass and **manure**.

Matter that has a lot of carbon is dry and brown. It includes paper and dry leaves.

DID YOU KNOW?

Never put meat, bones, or oil in your pile. It will smell bad, and raccoons and rats may get into it.

CHAPTER 3

LAYER UP

You can keep your pile in a **bin**. A bin should have good **drainage**.

compost bin

Put a layer of sticks on the bottom of your bin. This will drain extra water away from the pile. Layer the green and brown matter over the sticks.

grass clippings

paper

vegetable scraps

dry leaves

The first layer is brown. You can use paper and dry leaves.

The second is green. You can use table scraps and grass.

The third is brown, the next is green, and so on.

The pile should be about four to five feet tall (1.2 to 1.5 meters).

Add water to keep the pile moist.

Over the next few weeks your bin will heat up. The micro-organisms are at work!

The heat will break the matter down more quickly. The pile will get smaller. When this happens, it is time to turn and mix it.

Use a shovel or garden fork. Be sure to ask an adult before using gardening tools.

DID YOU KNOW?

Cover the pile to keep rain away. If the pile gets too wet, it won't get hot.

garden
fork

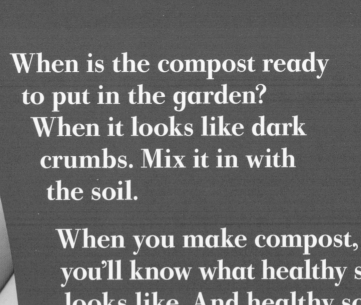

When is the compost ready to put in the garden? When it looks like dark crumbs. Mix it in with the soil.

When you make compost, you'll know what healthy soil looks like. And healthy soil makes a healthy garden. So give it a boost with compost. It's like a vitamin for your plants!

ACTIVITIES & TOOLS

COMPOST IN ACTION

Sure, turning your table scraps into compost may be great for the environment. But does it really make a difference to your plants? Let's see.

What You Need:
- two pots of the same size
- compost
- enough seeds to plant two pots
- soil

❶ Start with two pots of the same size. Put the same kind of soil in each pot.

❷ Plant the same kind of seeds in each pot.

❸ Add a little compost to the soil in one pot.

❹ Water your plants and put them in a sunny window. Make sure they receive the same amount of water and sunlight.

❺ Watch the plants grow. Measure them. Is one taller? Does one plant look stronger?

❻ Analyze your findings. Do they suggest that compost is good for plants?

GLOSSARY

carbon: An element found in nature.

compost: A mixture of matter that used to be alive (grass) or its products (paper) that is used to improve soil.

drainage: A bin's ability to let water run out, leaving it empty or dry.

humus: A dark material that forms a part of the soil and is the result of rotted plant or animal matter.

landfill: A system of garbage disposal in which the waste is buried between layers of earth.

manure: Bodily waste from farm animals like chickens and cows.

micro-organisms: Tiny life forms that you need a microscope to see.

nitrogen: An element that occurs as a gas.

organic matter: The remains of plants and animals and their waste products.

organisms: Living things, such as people, plants, or animals.

INDEX

TO LEARN MORE

Learning more is as easy as 1, 2, 3.

1) Go to www.factsurfer.com

2) Enter "composting" into the search box.

3) Click the "Surf" to see a list of websites.

With factsurfer, finding more information is just a click away.